11   WONDERFUL WORLD OF KNOWLEDGE

Disney's

Wonderful

World of

Knowledge

THE DANBURY PRESS

THE DANBURY PRESS

a division of Grolier Enterprises, Inc.

ROBERT B. CLARKE	*Publisher*
ROBERT G. BARTNER	*Marketing Director*
GILBERT EVANS	*Creative Director*
THE STONEHOUSE PRESS	*Production Supervision*

ARNOLDO MONDADORI EDITORE

MARIO GENTILINI	*Editor-in-Chief*
ELISA PENNA	*Supervising Editor*
GIOVAN BATTISTA CARPI CLAUDIO MAZZOLI	*Illustrators*
LUISA RIBOLZI	*Author*

"Disney's WONDERFUL WORLD OF KNOWLEDGE"
is an updated and enlarged English version of
an encyclopedia heretofore printed in the Italian language by
ARNOLDO MONDADORI EDITORE, MILAN
and entitled (in English Translation) "Disney ENCYCLOPEDIA"

CONTENTS

HOW HOLIDAYS BEGIN

Here we are, boys and girls, the pride of the Junior Woodchucks—Huey, Dewey, and Louie. We're here to take you on another exciting trip. Just hang onto our ducktails, and we'll whisk you across oceans and continents. We're going to show you how people all over the world celebrate holidays and festivals. You will see dragons dance through the streets on the Chinese New Year; brightly uniformed guardsmen march past the Queen of England during her birthday celebration; crowds of costumed merry-makers at Mardi Gras; and much, much more.

But before we start our journey, we would like to say a few words about how holidays got started. Holidays go back to prehistoric times, when we ducks first began to waddle across the earth. People in those days were very superstitious. They feared and worshiped the forces of nature—the sun and the moon, thunder and lightning. They believed in good and evil spirits. When they wanted help from nature, or to have the gods smile on them, they held some sort of ceremony. At harvest-time, or when the season changed, they also held special rites. Eventually these celebrations became yearly events.

Many of the first holidays had religious overtones. They were "holy days." Later, when countries were formed, people began to celebrate national holidays as well. For example, they would make a holiday out of their independence day or the birthday of one of their country's heroes.

Today all sorts of holidays—and holy days—are observed throughout the world. Some of them are solemn; others are gay. One holiday found just about everywhere is the weekly day of rest. This holiday goes back to biblical times. The Book of Genesis tells us that "God blessed the seventh day and hallowed it, because on it God rested from all his work which he had done in Creation."

Holidays serve an important purpose. They unite people in a common activity. It might be prayer, or a patriotic display, or just having a good time. Whatever the purpose, holidays help to strengthen a person's feelings toward his fellow men and women. And that's a very good thing—don't you agree?

Okay, boys and girls, now we're ready to begin our grand tour. Uncle Scrooge is going to make sure we have first-class travel arrangements. So follow us ducks—we're off!

9

*Some masked revelers off to join the Mummers'
Parade, Philadelphia's annual New Year's Day event.*

GREETING THE NEW YEAR

Church bells ring, horns toot, whistles blow, and brightly colored paper streamers fill the air. There's a lot of excitement as people say hello to the new year. It is one of the oldest and gayest customs celebrated all over the world. In Times Square in New York City and in Trafalgar Square in London, crowds gather to "watch the old year out," and "welcome the new year in." Of course, there are also many home parties and people wear fancy paper hats, blow toy horns, and throw confetti. Now that we three ducks are getting older, Uncle Donald lets us stay up until 1 minute after midnight on December 31 to join in the celebration. Huey, Dewey, and I usually have a glass of ginger ale with two cherries in it and

10

Rose Bowl Parade in Pasadena, California, a yearly New Year's Day event.

all the peanuts we can eat! Grandma Duck used to make sure we were tucked into bed before she left the house to join the New Year festivities held in Duckburg Square. But now that we're older, we don't have to miss the fun.

New Year's Day, the very first day of the calendar year, is a happy time, too. It is celebrated by grown-ups and children in almost every country throughout the world. Offices and businesses are closed, and there's never any school! People invite company to their homes, or they visit friends and relatives. And there are usually great things to eat at these parties. You ought to taste Grandma Duck's fruit cake! She uses an old family recipe and starts making the cake in October.

Lots of people in the United States spend New Year's Day watching special television programs. Our favorites are the Rose Bowl Parade in Pasadena, California, the championship football bowl games, and the Mummers Parade that is held every January 1st in Philadelphia, Pennsylvania. That's a lot of television for one day!

Many people make New Year's resolutions—promises to do better in the coming year. Last January 1st, Huey, Dewey, and I agreed to keep our room neat and not leave our socks on the floor. We kept our resolution, too—at least for a week. But we did keep our promise to Uncle Donald that we would work harder in school.

11

A caravan of camels plods along the banks of the Nile River in Egypt.

No holiday has ever been observed on so many different dates or in so many different ways as New Year's. Thousands of years ago our old friends the Egyptians celebrated the new year in the middle of June! This sounds like a strange thing to do, but they had a very good reason. You see, this was the time of year when the Nile River usually overflowed its banks. The extra water was used for the thirsty crops. Naturally, all of this water helped the crops to grow and this meant that there would be plenty of food for the coming year. That's a pretty good reason to celebrate! The ancient Greeks began their year when the new moon rose, sometime after June 21. In most European countries during the Middle Ages the new year began on March 25, the day of the Feast of the Annunciation.

Some countries still observe New

These cheerful creatures lead the Chinese Lunar New Year's parade in New York City's Chinatown.

Year's Day on different dates. It all depends on the calendars they use. The Chinese have followed the lunar calendar for about 4,000 years. Their New Year festivities begin with the new moon in January and last until the next full moon, occurring sometime in February. So if you should happen to be visiting friends in China during that period, you can enjoy an extra New Year's celebration.

And what a celebration it is! Almost everyone stays up all night on New Year's Eve. Only the little children are in bed. But they make up for it, because they're always up in time to enjoy the large family dinner that is eaten during the early morning festivities. On New Year's Day, the gods and ancestors are greeted in prayer and their blessings are asked. There are colorful New Year's Day parades in many of the large cities of China as well as in Chinese communities throughout the world. Huey, Dewey, and I have heard so much about these parades—especially the dragons. But don't be frightened. We don't mean real dragons. You all know there isn't such a thing as a real, live dragon. Instead, many paraders form a

13

line and drape a long, brightly colored cloth over their heads and shoulders. It looks something like a great big caterpillar. What makes it look so different, though, is the carved dragon's head. It can be made of either wood or papier-mâché, and it usually has big scary eyes, large ears, and a huge angry mouth with long, sharp fangs! You can almost imagine great streams of fire pouring out of the monster's mouth. The person who leads the dragon's body through the streets has the honor of wearing the ferocious head or of carrying it on a pole. You see, boys and girls, sometimes the cloth body of the dragon is also supported by poles, which are carried by the paraders. As the dragon makes its way down the street, it weaves in and out of the parade, almost attacking the onlookers! It's all done in fun, though, and everyone laughs and applauds as the dragon passes by.

The traditional Chinese dragon performs its duties with the help of the men supporting it with poles.

14

This be-ribboned straw horse is a popular Japanese New Year's decoration.

Another wonderful part of the Chinese New Year's celebration is the great fireworks display. You might have to hold your ears because there's an awful lot of noise. In the old days, the popping of firecrackers was supposed to scare away the demons, or bad spirits. Today, of course, it's just all part of the festivities.

For the next few days of the New Year's celebration, friends and relatives visit one another and exchange gifts. Children usually receive little red envelopes filled with money. Dewey told Uncle Scrooge about this lovely custom, but he didn't seem very interested.

Throughout the Orient, New Year's Day is looked upon as a day to make a fresh start. Houses are cleaned from top to bottom until everything shines. Everyone makes sure that he's paid all of his old debts, and dresses up in his newest clothes.

New Year's Day in Japan is an exciting

16

holiday for everyone. We three ducks would really enjoy being with our Japanese friends on December 31, because their New Year's celebration lasts for a whole week! They decorate their houses with wreaths of pine branches, sprays of Japanese apricot, and bamboo shoots—all symbols of a long and healthy life. The *shime-nawa*, a straw braid decorated with strips of white paper, is hung over the doorway to keep evil spirits away. During the festive New Year week, the boys and girls have their own way of celebrating. They organize kite-flying parties. The sky is filled with special kites in the shapes of fish, dragons, butterflies, and dragonflies.

Tet Nguyendan is the name given to the Vietnamese New Year festival. The holiday is celebrated during the first 7 days of the first month of the lunar calendar. Like the Chinese New Year, it may fall anytime between January 21 and February 19. It is a time for parades, fancy costumes, fireworks, and fun. The Vietnamese believe that whatever happens during the Tet holiday—happy times or sad times—is a sign of what the rest of the year will be like.

The people of Ethiopia celebrate the new year in early September, when the heavy rains have stopped and the harvest season begins. On New Year's Eve, the men and young boys of the villages gather bundles of branches. When the sun goes down, the men carefully set fire to the branches. With these brightly lit torches, the men and boys make their way through the village, stopping at every house to sing a happy New Year's song. Many of the people come out of their houses to join in the singing.

On New Year's Day, the little girls in the Ethiopian villages gather bouquets of beautiful flowers. Dressed in fancy costumes, the girls carry their bouquets from house to house, singing and bringing good wishes for the New Year.

Iran celebrates New Year's Day on March 21, just in time for the arrival of spring. For 2 weeks before this exciting holiday, musicians and dancers perform in the city streets, and everyone stops to watch them.

On the Wednesday before New Year's Day, families build a small bonfire in front of their homes. If everyone jumps across the fire, the coming year will be filled with good fortune. Just watch your feathers—and feet!

For 12 days after New Year's Day, everyone dresses in their newest clothes and visits friends and relatives. Grandma Duck would certainly enjoy this custom. She always likes an excuse to get a new spring outfit! The children of Iran receive gifts, usually coins and sweets.

New Year's Day has religious meaning to the Jews, Hindus, and Muslims. Rosh Hashanah, which means "the head of the year," is New Year's Day in the Hebrew calendar. It may fall at anytime between the end of September and the beginning of October. Religious services are held in synagogues throughout the world. After the services, families often gather together for a holiday dinner.

Each of the two main religious groups in India—the Muslims and the Hindus—has its own date for the celebration of the new year. It may fall on a different day each year. There are a variety of different religious groups among the Hindus. Each of these groups considers a different date as the beginning of the year. One Hindu new year, Baisakhi, comes sometime in April or May.

The Muslims observe the beginning of the year on the 10th day of Muharram, the first month of the Muslim year.

Opposite page: A bonfire lights the sky at the Maskal Festival in Addis Ababa, capital of Ethiopia.
Top of page: Epiphany celebration in Ethiopia.

HAPPY NEW YEAR IN OTHER LANDS

Today most countries celebrate the new year on January 1. This custom started during the 1500's when the Gregorian calendar, the one we use today, was first introduced. January, the first month of the year, was named after Janus. He was the Roman god of gates and doors and of beginnings and endings. Janus had two faces. One face looked ahead while the other looked backward. When Dewey heard about this, he thought up a joke. He said that Janus could see himself coming and going!

And speaking of going, how about a trip through some of the countries in Europe to see how New Year's Eve and New Year's Day are celebrated? Our first stop is Germany. On New Year's Eve people in many towns and villages gather together to look into the future. They have an ancient practice, which they still follow today, to help them predict coming events. A large tub filled with cold water is placed in the middle of the room. Molten lead (hot, liquid lead) is then poured into the tub and the shape that the lead takes while it floats in the water tells what the future will bring. This is one experiment that we three ducks will have to try if we ever come across any molten lead.

Families in many countries—Italy, Portugal, and the Netherlands, among others —begin the new year by attending church services. Later in the day neighbors and friends visit with one another, exchanging gifts and food. We've been told that in Italy, the young girls and boys receive gifts of money on New Year's Day. Some children dress up in colorful costumes and go from door to door asking for candy or cakes, as we do on Halloween.

Grandma Duck told us about an old New Year's belief that still exists today in Scotland, and parts of England and Germany. It's called "first-footing." The people in these countries watch closely to see who will be the very first person to enter their house on New Year's Day. If it is a dark-haired man, it is believed that he brings good luck to the household— particularly if he's carrying presents! We're not sure this always works, but it's worth a try!

In both Scotland and France, January 1 is a time of gift giving, parties, and visits with friends. Everybody is welcome!

You can see, boys and girls, no matter when or where New Year's Day is celebrated, it is always a day worth remembering. So, with a toot of our horns and a flutter of our feathers, we'd like to wish you a happy, cheerful New Year!

Scotsmen, skirling their bagpipes, parade in
traditional dress.

21

RELIGIOUS HOLIDAYS

Now it's time, just for a change, for us to get a little serious. (Bet you didn't think we could do that!) That's because we're going to take a look at a group of holidays that have deep meaning for people around the world. They're the ones that have kept the original sense of the word "holiday"—the holy days, or religious holidays. Each faith has set aside its own special days.

EASTER TIME

Let's start right off by talking about the most important religious holiday in the Christian calendar—Easter—the day that celebrates Christ's resurrection. Though Easter itself always falls on the first Sunday after the first full moon following March 21, it's really more a season than a single day.

The season starts with the solemn 40-day period called Lent, which begins on Ash Wednesday. On Ash Wednesday, Roman Catholics (and some Episcopa-

Easter services at the Greek Orthodox Church of the Holy Sepulcher in Jerusalem.

lians and Lutherans) go to church, where they receive a mark of ashes on their foreheads. The ashes are supposed to serve as a visible reminder that human life ends in death. Lent is marked by prayer and by observing certain rules of fasting.

Shrove Tuesday, just before Lent begins, has become a day of feasting and fun in many places around the world. It ends a period called carnival, which is a time of merrymaking or "letting off steam" before the serious preparations for Easter start. We'll tell you all about the various carnival celebrations, such as Mardi Gras and Fasching, later on. But right now we'd just like to say that *we'd* like to spend next Shrove Tuesday in the little English town of Olney. They have a special tradition there that we think is a terrific idea—the ladies' pancake race. As the ladies dash toward the finish line, they flip pancakes into the air from their skillets! We'd like to be there just in case they drop any. We'd be ready and waiting with butter and syrup. (We believe in being prepared, you see, if we're going to do a lot of fasting during Lent—though the hot cross buns and other cakes eaten during Lent are delicious, too!)

HOLY WEEK

The last week of Lent is known as Holy Week. It begins on Palm Sunday, when palm branches are handed out in church. They commemorate Christ's entry into Jerusalem, when his path was strewn with palm branches. (In many European countries, other kinds of branches are also used.)

Some European cities have special events during Holy Week. One of the most beautiful takes place in the Spanish city of Seville. Every night processions called *pasos* move through the streets, with muscians, singers, and floats depicting scenes from the Passion of Christ. ("Passion" is the word that is used for Christ's suffering and death.) The processions end at the Cathedral, which is one of the largest and most beautiful in Europe.

Then, far to the north, in Germany, Holy Week is time for the Oberammergau Passion Play. Oberammergau is a small town in the mountains of Bavaria. In 1633 it was threatened by a terrible plague that was devastating the countryside. The villagers took a vow that if they survived they would perform the

Passion of Christ every year. Now the passion play is held every 10 years, as it has been since 1680. Almost everyone in Oberammergau takes part—if not as actors, then as stagehands, ticket sellers, and so on. Of course, the greatest honor is to be chosen for the role of Christ.

Holy Week draws to a close on Good Friday, the day that marks Christ's crucifixion, and then finally, it's Easter Sunday. Easter itself is celebrated in church, often at a sunrise service. That tradition comes from the ancient spring festivals that marked the "return" of the sun after the long, hard winter was over.

Many people have new clothes that they like to show off in an "Easter parade"—there's even a song about it. One of the most famous takes place on New York City's Fifth Avenue, where women try to outdo each other by wearing fantastic hats and their best spring finery.

Besides our delicious Easter dinner (our favorite is baked ham), we're looking forward to the arrival of the Easter bunny. Nobody knows when or where he was born, but he's popular in many countries. He makes us work hard, though, looking for the colorful dyed Easter eggs he hides around the house.

Eggs, by the way, are an Easter symbol because they stand for new life. Coloring Easter eggs is something we share with boys and girls in many countries. In Eastern Europe, especially Russia and Poland, the eggs are painted in beautiful designs that have special meanings. Some coun-

Opposite page: Medieval walls surround Avila, Spain, a city notable for its Holy Week processions. Boys and girls wear white or green veils (such as shown top of page) and carry palms that have been blessed. Right: Holy Week procession in Guatemala. Religious statues are carried through the streets at this time.

tries have egg-knocking contests (hard-boiled eggs, of course!), and the winner is the one whose egg stays unbroken. We can't wait for Duckburg's annual egg-rolling contest. Of course, it's much smaller than the one held on the White House lawn in Washington, D.C., but we think it's just as much fun.

ASCENSION DAY AND PENTECOST

The 40th day after Easter—which is always a Thursday—is called Ascension Day. It celebrates Christ's rising, or ascension, into heaven. Ascension Day is one of the oldest celebrations of Christianity, and it has been observed since the 4th century A.D.

Pentecost comes 10 days later, or 50 days after Easter. (In its original Greek, *pentekost* means "50th day.") It is one of the most important of Christian religious holidays.

Pentecost marks the Holy Spirit's gift of faith to the apostles and disciples, and so it is considered the beginning of Christianity. In England and in countries first settled by the English, the day is called Whitsunday. Long ago, new Christians were baptized on Pentecost, and wore white garments for the ceremony. "White Sunday" eventually became "Whitsunday."

27

SAINTS' DAYS

Many festivals are linked to the Christian saints. We've already told you about some of them in other parts of this book. Now we want to talk to you about some holidays that honor patron saints—saints that protect a particular country or city. There are so many patron saints we hardly know where to begin. In some countries of Europe and South America, every town and village has a different patron saint. Why, there are countries where there's at least one saint's festival every week!

One of the most colorful saints was Saint George, the patron saint of England. His greatest deed of bravery took place while he was traveling through the Middle East. One day he came upon a town that was threatened by a terrible dragon. Saint George offered to fight the dragon. With his powerful sword Ascalon he succeeded in capturing the great beast. Tying it up, he dragged it into the town. He told the people to follow the Christian faith and then he baptized 20,000 of them. When that was done, he cut off the dragon's head with one mighty blow.

Later Saint George was martyred by the Romans. Because he was a Christian, he was tortured and beheaded. But the memory of his bravery lived on. When King Richard I of England went off to the Crusades in A.D. 1190, he put England under the protection of Saint George. For centuries after that, English soldiers went into battle with the cry, "For England and Saint George!"

Icon (religious painting on wood) showing Saint George slaying the dragon.

29

Each year on September 19, the people of Naples hold a 3-day festival in honor of San Gennaro (Saint Januarius), their patron saint. (There is a similar ceremony in New York City, which has a large southern Italian population.) An effigy of the saint is paraded through the street in a great procession. But the most important part of the festival takes place in the great cathedral of Naples. Here are preserved the skull of the martyred saint and small bottles containing his blood.

Now before we tell you what happens to the blood during the festival, we must go back to the year A.D. 305. San Gennaro, a native of Naples, was then a bishop. Like many other Christians in those days, he was killed by the Romans because of his religious beliefs. But it wasn't easy to kill San Gennaro. It is said that the Romans first threw him into a furnace that had been heated for 3 days. But he escaped from that unharmed. Then they took him to a great arena and let loose

Bright lights and crowds of happy people fill the streets during the Feast of San Gennaro.

Saint John's Eve in Finland.

ferocious lions. But none of the lions would go near the saint. Finally the Romans beheaded him.

An old woman who was present when the saint was killed picked up some of his blood in two containers. The skull was also saved. The blood eventually caked up into solid form. But an amazing thing happened when the blood was brought near the skull. It immediately turned back into a liquid. The miracle of San Gennaro's blood has occurred thousands of times over the centuries. It happens each year during the festival. No one has ever been able to explain why. But the Neopolitan people believe that if the miracle does not occur their city will have a bad year.

In 1799, during the Napoleonic Wars, a French army occupied Naples. The general commanding the French troops heard a rumor that the priests were telling the people that the miracle would not happen that year. It was said that the priests hoped this news would stir the people to revolt against the French. On the day of San Gennaro's festival, the French commander appeared at the cathedral. The hour came for the miracle to occur, but the blood remained in a solid state. The French general sent a message to the bishop: "If the blood does not become liquid in five minutes I will order my cannon to bombard the city." Before the five minutes were up, the blood turned to liquid and the people of Naples cheered and shouted for joy.

A saint's festival that is popular all over Europe is Saint John's Eve. It is observed on June 23, the night before Saint John the Baptist's birthday. (It's the only saint's day that marks the birth of a saint. All the other saints' days mark the day of their death or martyrdom.) Saint John 31 is the patron saint of Puerto Rico. His festival, which is also known as Midsummer Eve, falls on the longest day of the year. In pagan times, people worshiped the sun, and so the longest day was a time of festivity.

Midsummer Eve is still celebrated in Europe. In many countries, people light giant bonfires and dance around them until the early morning hours. In Austria, France, and Finland the bonfires are often built on hilltops. Spanish people sometimes build them in the streets of their cities.

ALL SAINTS' AND ALL SOULS' DAYS

On All Saints' Day, November 1, Catholics honor all the saints, especially those for whom there is no special observance. The evening before, Halloween, is the fun part—but we'll get to that later.

November 2 is All Souls' Day. In the Catholic Church, masses are said for the souls of the faithful.

THE EAST

One of the main religions of far-off Asia is Buddhism. The religious holidays in the Buddhist calendar vary from country to country, and they also vary according to which sect, or branch, of Buddhism a person belongs to.

An important Buddhist religious holiday is the 3-day spring festival called Wesak. Celebrated at the time of the full moon in April or May, it marks the Buddha's birthday. Food and money are given to the poor, and homes are decorated with lovely flower garlands and lanterns. People go to the temples to pray

32

and to bring offerings of flowers. This is how the people of Thailand, Burma, and Ceylon observe Wesak. Thailand also celebrates the Visakha Puja festival, in which 1,250 candles are lit in the royal temple. The candles stand for the original number of monks chosen by the Buddha.

Buddhists in China and Japan also observe the Buddha's birthday and those of his principal followers. Flowers, lanterns, and even theatrical performances are part of the celebrations.

The chief religion of India is Hinduism, and many Hindu religious holidays

Above: Lights gleam and flicker in every Indian city and village during Divali, a religious holiday. Opposite page: Indian woman decorates her floor with a design made of rice flour in honor of Divali. The small shallow clay dishes at the corners and in the center of the design are called Chirags. They are filled with kerosene and a wick made of twisted cotton that is lit. The purpose of the lighting is to guide Lakshmi, goddess of wealth and prosperity, into the home. Families are afraid that the goddess might overlook a home that is dark.

are dedicated to the gods Siva and Vishnu. Most Hindu gods exist in many incarnations, or forms, and there are festivals for each. The 5-day spring festival of Holi honors different gods in different parts of India. Bonfires and parades are held, and people throw colored powders at each other. In the fall most Hindus celebrate Divali, which is also called the Festival of Lights.

RAMADAN

Now let's take a hop over to the Middle East, where the Muslim faith began many years ago and where most of the world's Muslims still live today.

Fasting is one of the five basic parts of the Muslim faith, or Islam. And a special period called Ramadan—the ninth month of the Muslim calendar—has been set aside for fasting. During Ramadan, Muslims fast only during the day; they are allowed to eat and drink at night. In the Koran, the Muslim holy book, the rule goes this way: ". . . eat and drink until so much of the dawn appears that a white thread may be distinguished from a black; then keep the fast completely until night."

The end of Ramadan is called Id-al-Fitr. This is a happy time, and after prayers in the mosque, people dress in their best clothes and there are parties and visits with family and friends.

JEWISH HOLIDAYS

Judaism—the oldest of the world's three main religions—also began in the Middle East thousands of years ago. Today Jews live in every country of the world. Observance of the Jewish holidays forms a link among all Jews, wherever they may be.

Muslim women in Cairo, Egypt, praying on the last day of Ramadan. Ramadan is a solemn holiday lasting *for a month. During this period daily activities are kept to a minimum.*

35

The most solemn, serious day in the Jewish calendar is Yom Kippur, the Day of Atonement. This holy day usually falls in early October, 10 days after Rosh Hashanah, the Jewish New Year, which we talked about before. It is the day on which Jews pray for forgiveness for their sins of the past year. The observance of Yom Kippur, which lasts from one sundown to the next, includes fasting, prayers in the synagogue, and remembrance of the dead.

Early spring brings Purim, a happy, merry holiday that's a favorite with Jewish children. Purim celebrates the time in the 5th century B.C. when Queen Esther of Persia, who was Jewish, stopped the evil prime minister Haman from carrying out his plan to kill the Persian Jews. The children get to make a lot of noise during services in temple. As the Purim story is read, every time Haman's name is mentioned, they shake a special noisemaker called a grogger as hard as they can.

Maybe we'll be able to go to a Purim party. Everyone might dress up in costumes representing Queen Esther, Haman, or the other characters in the story. There'll be delicious, three-cornered pastries called hamantaschen—they're supposed to look like Haman's hat.

Spring also brings Passover, which celebrates the Jews being freed from slavery in Egypt, according to the description in the Bible. Passover is marked by services in the synagogue and by a special family dinner called a Seder. Each dish that is served has a special meaning. Best-known is the flat, crisp, cracker known as matzo. It is a reminder of the unleavened bread —baked without yeast—that was all the Jews had time to take with them when they fled Egypt.

At the Seder table, everyone takes turns

A Jewish family celebrates Passover with a Seder, a dinner at which special foods are served. The father is reading from the Haggadah, a book that tells the story of Passover.

are Shabuoth, or the Feast of Weeks, which comes in the spring, 50 days after the second day of Passover, and Succoth, which falls in September and October. During Succoth, little huts are built out of branches and decorated with flowers and plants that stand for the harvest. The huts are supposed to be like the ones the Jews lived in in the wilderness.

Finally, in the winter (usually in December), we come to Hanukkah. This joyous holiday commemorates the Jews' victory over armies of the Syrian king Antiochus IV, in the 2nd century B.C.

Hanukkah is also called the Festival of Lights, and candles are placed in an nine-branched candleholder called a menorah. When the Jews defeated the Syrians, they were able to return to their temple in Jerusalem. They wanted to rededicate the temple and make it a holy place again, but they had only enough sacred oil to burn on the altar for 1 night. It would take a week to make more. Then, by a miracle, the oil burned for 8 nights. So today one candle is lit the first night of Hanukkah, two the second, and so on. On the last night, eight candles burn brightly in the menorah.

Hanukkah is a happy holiday, with presents, parties, and games played with tops called dreidels.

'TIS THE SEASON

Here we are in December, heading for one of the best holidays of all—Christmas! In Duckburg, we think that Christmas means snow and sleighbells, but in some parts of the world it's warm now, and below the equator it's summertime.

Everyone knows that the peak of the Christmas season comes on December 24 and December 25 and that this joyous

reading the Passover story from a book called the Haggadah. Special songs are sung, and the youngest child in the family is allowed to ask the "four questions"— which begin "Why is this night different from all other nights?" The answers explain the meaning of Passover. The holiday really lasts for 8 days.

Two Jewish holidays we'd like to mention originated as harvest festivals. They

37

holiday celebrates the birth of Christ. But some Christmas traditions may not be so familiar to us.

In some countries Christmas begins about a month earlier, with a period known as Advent (from the Latin word for "coming"). And it ends on January 6, which is called Epiphany or Twelfth Night. That was the day on which the Three Wise Man, or Magi, came out of the East bringing their gifts to the infant Jesus. That's why January 6 is the night for giving gifts in many places around the world.

Santa Lucia Day in Sweden.

In northern European countries, children start their Advent calendars on December 1. An Advent calendar has 25 little windows that can be opened to reveal pictures of Christmas gifts, scenes from fairy tales, or Bible stories. It's

tempting to open all the windows at once, but it's much more fun to enjoy the surprises one by one. Behind the last window, which is the largest, there is usually a Nativity scene or a picture of the infant Jesus.

In some parts of Germany, Advent is marked by an Advent house. This miniature wood or papier-mâché house has four colored windows with candles behind them. One candle is lit each week of Advent.

In Sweden some people use a special candleholder with white candles called "living lights." In the long, dark northern winter, light means warmth and joy—and before we forget, let's talk about a special Swedish custom that glows with these feelings.

Santa Lucia Day, December 13, marks the beginning of Christmastime in Sweden. We don't really know how this saint, who was born in Italy, got to faraway Sweden. But it may be because the name Lucia means "light," and long ago, when Christianity came to Sweden, December 13 was thought to be the shortest, darkest day of the year.

Anyway, here's how the day is celebrated. Early in the morning, while everyone else is still asleep (or pretending to be asleep), all the girls in the family put on long white robes and crowns of leaves topped by lighted candles. Singing as they go, the girls move from room to room. They serve coffee and delicious "Lucia" buns to all the older members of the family, starting with their parents. The grownups say there's no nicer way to be awakened!

After Santa Lucia Day, everyone can enjoy Christmas cake and gingerbread, and sometimes even the children are allowed a tiny sip of glogg—a delicious hot drink made with red wine, sugar, and cinnamon.

FROM SAINT NICHOLAS
TO SANTA CLAUS

We already know a lot about Santa Claus, so let's turn things around and take a look at the original Saint Nicholas.

He must be pretty busy, too, since he's the patron saint of children, sailors, mer-

chants, Greece, and Russia. He lived in the 4th century A.D. and was bishop of Myra, in Asia Minor. There are many stories about his generosity. Perhaps the most famous concerns a man too poor to give his three daughters the dowries they needed in order to get married. One night Saint Nicholas secretly left a large bag of gold coins in their house—which also made him the patron saint of single girls!

In the Netherlands and Belgium, it is still Sinter Klaas (with his assistant Black Peter) who brings gifts to children on his day, December 6. The Dutch first brought the saint to America, where his name slowly changed from Sinter Klaas to Santa Claus.

DECK THE HALLS

Well, it's Christmas Eve at last, and tomorrow's the day! Of course Christmas wasn't always celebrated on December 25, because no one knows the exact date of Christ's birth. But the date was set once and for all in the 4th century A.D.

Christmas is a family holiday. Homes are made warm and bright with decorations. Besides the Christmas tree, we hang pine and holly wreaths on doors and over the mantel. Candles and lights shine brightly, and Christmas stars and bells are fun to put up too.

43

In Denmark birch twigs are decorated with small red apples and tiny figures of elf-like creatures called *nisser*. In Norway and Sweden, small straw objects—mostly animals—tied with red ribbons are popular. Straw is used because Jesus lay in a manger filled with straw. It also symbolizes food for the animals during the hard northern winter. In Norway even the birds have a Christmas! On farms they receive a bale of hay, and in the cities birdseed is put out for them. In fact, in many countries animals are given extra portions of food on this happy day.

Speaking of food, we can hardly wait for our wonderful Christmas dinner! It might be a big roast turkey with all the trimmings or Uncle Scrooge's favorite— a large roast beef. And there are European favorites, too, such as crisp roast goose or crunchy baked ham. And the desserts! We'll taste them all, from mince pie to English plum pudding to German *stollen* to hundreds of different kinds of cakes and cookies. . . . Gosh, aren't you getting hungry?

Left: *A 12th-century bas-relief by Bonanno Pisano showing shepherds sounding their horns as they approach the manger. Below: A representation of the Nativity scene in the stable at Bethlehem. Opposite page: Christmas goodies for a happy holiday.*

PRESENTS UNDER THE TREE

At our house we open our presents after dinner on Christmas Day. Of course every family has its own time for opening gifts. But until that great moment arrives, Huey, Dewey, and I, have a tough time. We can hardly stand it, trying to guess what's inside those brightly wrapped packages.

But wait a minute! Let's talk about the Christmas tree itself. No one knows ex-actly when or where this custom started. But long, long ago many people, particu-larly in northern Europe, believed that spirits lived in nature. Those in evergreen trees were especially important. Some-times these trees would be decorated to please their spirits. After the spread of Christianity, this custom was taken over as a way of honoring Christ. The Christ-mas tree we know, bright with ornaments, tinsel, and lights, caught on in many countries after the 18th century.

And the Yule log is still popular too.   47

"The stockings were hung by the chimney with care, In hopes that St. Nicholas soon would be there."

It's a large log (or a whole tree trunk) that's lit before Christmas and kept burning all during the festivities. It's supposed to bring good luck. We like what the French do with their Yule log—a rich, log-shaped chocolate cake called *bûche de noël!*

48

ALL KINDS OF CHRISTMASES

While we're busy opening our presents, let's take a look at a few more Christmas customs around the world.

In Great Britain and many countries

An expectant group of children in Mexico await the breaking of the piñata *with its shower of presents.*

first settled by the British, children receive their gifts from Father Christmas. He's a close relative of our Santa Claus—really a first cousin! Can you imagine how he must feel in such countries as Australia and New Zealand, where December 25 falls in the middle of hot summer? Poor Father Christmas, carrying all those heavy packages and wearing his warm red suit!

In France presents are sometimes brought by Père Noël, whose name means Father Christmas. In Sweden and Norway this important job is done by the Jultomten or the Jule-Nisse. These busy Christmas elves like to make sure that children have been good all year, so they always check with the parents before giving out gifts. (But have there ever been any bad children at Christmastime?)

In some Latin American and Mediterranean countries, it's the infant Jesus who brings the Christmas gifts. Children even put out food for his little donkey to eat. But Santa Claus is pretty well-known in these countries, too.

In Latin America too, especially in Mexico, children enjoy the Christmas *piñata*. This clay or papier-mâché jug, filled with candy and small gifts, is hung overhead. The children are blindfolded and given three turns to swing at the *piñata*. When it finally breaks, candies and gifts shower down and there's an excited scramble.

We could really go on talking about this wonderful holiday forever—or at least till next Christmas—but let's get ready for a different kind of holiday.

49

HOLIDAYS THAT REMEMBER PEOPLE

Huey and Dewey just had a bright idea. They think we should go through the entire calendar and find the holidays that remember people. You know there are holidays that remember all kinds of people—gods and goddesses, kings and queens, presidents, explorers, saints, and even sinners. But Huey and Dewey say that, as usual, I'm holding you up with my chatter. They want to start turning the pages of the calendar this very minute.

WINTER HOLIDAYS THAT REMEMBER PEOPLE

In the United States the birthdays of several famous men are celebrated in the winter. Some of the best-known are our first president George Washington; our 16th president, Abraham Lincoln; and the great civil rights leader, the Reverend Martin Luther King, Jr. King's birthday is on January 15th. On that day schools are closed in some cities, and people hold special programs to remember the work

George Washington

the Reverend King did to help the black people and the poor people win a better life.

Both Lincoln's and Washington's birthday are celebrated in February. Washington was born on February 22, and Lincoln's birthday is the 12th. Huey, Dewey, and I like to eat a cake shaped like a log on Lincoln's birthday to remind us that Honest Abe was born in a log cabin.

On the third Monday in February, we celebrate the birthday of our first president, George Washington. On that day we eat a cherry pie to remember the story about the time young George is supposed to have cut down a cherry tree. Some people say that when his father asked him who had cut the tree down George said, "I cannot tell a lie, Father. I cut down the cherry tree." Huey and Dewey say I shouldn't forget to tell you that Washington's birthday is a legal holiday in almost all of the United States. Schools, banks, and offices are closed. Special services are held at Washington's home, Mount Vernon, and at the Washington Monument in Washington, D.C.

St. Patrick's Day parade on New York City's Fifth Avenue.

CELEBRATIONS IN SPRINGTIME

Two saints who lived in the British Isles hundreds and hundreds of years ago are remembered on holidays in March. On March 1st the people of Wales celebrate their national holiday, which is named for their patron saint, David, or Dewi in Welsh. On this special day Welshmen wear a leek—a kind of small onion—in their buttonhole, and Welsh women wear a daffodil.

On March 17th, Huey, Dewey, and I like to be in one of the big cities like Dublin, Ireland, or New York City where many Irish people live. This is because March 17th is St. Patrick's Day. The day remembers the patron saint of Ireland. He was a teacher who helped set up many schools and churches. In Ireland, St. Patrick's Day is a great national holiday. In other parts of the world, Irish people and their friends celebrate by wearing something green. They also often wear little four-leaf clovers called shamrocks. In many cities there are great parades with lots of marching bands.

A little more than a month later on April 22nd, the people of the Soviet Union celebrate the birthday of Lenin. Lenin was a leader of the Russian Revo-

Trooping the Colour, London, England.

lution in 1917, and he was the first head of the Soviet Union.

On the second Sunday in May the streets in many towns in France are decorated to honor the memory of Saint Joan of Arc. Saint Joan is the French national heroine because she led the French against the English in the 15th century. She was taken **prisoner** by the English and burned at the **stake**. More than 500 years later she was made a saint.

June brings a holiday that makes Huey, Dewey, and me very jealous. It is the official birthday celebration of the king or queen of England. You see, the kings and queens of England have two birthday parties. One is on their real birthday, whenever that happens to be. The other is held in June because the weather is usually lovely in England at that time, and everyone can join in the fun. An exciting military show called Trooping the Colour is held, and military bands play marching songs. The king or queen, dressed in a scarlet jacket, sits on horseback to watch the troops go by. The streets of London are lined with people cheering their ruler.

On June 23, in the tiny European Duchy of Luxembourg, the people celebrate their national holiday. It honors their ruler the Grand Duke. The capital city, which is also called Luxembourg, is full of bright flags and beautiful flowers on this little nation's biggest holiday.

53

The only public holiday for royalty in the United States is held in Hawaii, on June 11 or 12, to honor the former king Kamehameha I. On this colorful state holiday, parades and public picnics are held. At the picnics or *luaus*, as they are called, Huey, Dewey, and I ate delicious fish, a tasty dish called *poi*, and roast pig. We all wore yellow flowers on Kamehameha Day because yellow was the color of Hawaiian royalty.

Kamehameha Day, Oahu, Hawaii.

July brings the birthdays of two men who have played an important role in different parts of the world.

On July 23, the people of Ethiopia celebrate the birthday of their leader. He is known as Haile Selassie I, Emperor of Ethiopia, King of Kings, Elect of God, and Conquering Lion of Judah. Legend has it that Haile Selassie is descended from the Bible's King Solomon and the Queen of Sheba. On his special day the Ethiopian

Dussehra Festival, Delhi, India.

Emperor stands on the balcony of his palace in the capital city Addis Ababa and proudly accepts the greetings of the thousands of Ethiopians who have come to wish him a happy birthday.

Half way around the world, on July 24th, South Americans celebrate the birthday of Simón Bolívar. Bolívar, who lived at the beginning of the 19th century, was a statesman and a general who helped many South American countries to win their freedom from Spanish rule. Bolívar is sometimes called "the Washington of South America." The celebration of his birthday is especially colorful in the city where he was born—Caracas, Venezuela.

Huey, Dewey, and I once made a very exciting trip to India in October. We were just in time for the Dussehra Festival in Delhi. We saw great big demons like those in the picture above. Aren't they ferocious? Dussehra is a Hindu festival that celebrates the victory of good over evil. But we missed a fine August holiday —the birthday of the beloved Indian god Krishma. The holiday is called Janmastami and lasts for 2 days. On his birthday people put little brass or plaster dolls made to look like Krishna in a cradle decorated with flowers, and they go to their temples.

55

FALL HOLIDAYS FOR SAINTS, SINNERS, EXPLORERS, AND STATESMEN

In the month of October, Huey, Dewey, and I remember two great explorers from Europe who helped to put the Americas on the map. On October 8th in Norway, and in some parts of the United States, people celebrate the memory of Leif Ericson. Ericson was the Viking sailor who led an expedition to North America about A.D. 1000. Some people say he founded Vinland (Wineland), the first colony in North America. But no one is quite sure after so many years where the colony was, because it has disappeared.

On October 12th, 1492, Christopher Columbus, an Italian seaman sailing for the Spanish, discovered America. Huey and Dewey, who know all kinds of strange facts, say that the anniversary of Columbus's discovery of America became a legal holiday in the United States in 1892. It is now celebrated on the second Monday in October. Columbus Day is also celebrated in Puerto Rico, parts of Canada, and in some cities in Italy and Spain.

October 26th is the birthday of one of the most important modern rulers, the Shah Mohammed Riza Pahlavi of Iran. On that day the Shah's beautiful capital city of Teheran is made even more gorgeous with brilliantly decorated flags, and all Iranians honor their "King of Kings."

Most days that remember people, as you can see, recall the births and deaths, the deeds and sacrifices of great men. On Guy Fawkes Day—November 5th—Englishmen remember a horrible act that took place on that day in 1605. It has gone down in English history as the "Gun-

Above and below: Anniversary celebration in Persapolis, Iran, commemorating the founding of the Persian Empire.
Opposite page: Christopher Columbus.

The Scottish countryside resounds with the music of the bagpipes on St. Andrew's Day.

powder Plot." Guy Fawkes, Robert Catesby, Thomas Percy, and some other men buried 36 barrels of gunpowder in the cellar of the House of Lords. They were going to set off the explosion on November 5th, the day the Houses of Parliament were to open officially. The explosion would have killed King James I, and all the members of Parliament. Fortunately, the plot was discovered in time. The King and all the others were saved. Guy Fawkes and the other men who plotted with him were tried, found guilty, and executed. The day the plot was discovered was made a national holiday. On that day people all over England build huge bonfires and burn effigies—stuffed figures—of Guy Fawkes and the other "Gunpowder Plot" villains.

A much different kind of holiday is held in China on November 12th. That is the birthday of Sun Yat-sen, the founder of the Republic of China. His birthday is now a national holiday and

58

all schools, banks, and many businesses are closed in his memory. Four days later, on November 16th, the people of Sweden remember one of their greatest leaders, King Gustavus Adolphus, who died in the battle of Lützen in 1632.

November 30th is a happy day in Scotland because it is the feast of Saint Andrew, Scotland's patron saint. His day is celebrated by Scottish people wherever they may be. It is a time for happiness and gay parties. On this day the featured dish is haggis, a pudding that is made of the heart and other organs of a sheep or a calf. "Piping in the Haggis" is a ceremony that is particularly observed on Saint Andrew's Day. (Huey and Dewey, who have all those facts in their heads, say the Scottish people like to have haggis on New Year's Eve, too!) Men dressed in kilts and tartans set their bagpipes skirling, and all the assembled people sing the songs of Scotland's great poet, Robert Burns. Then the trays of haggis are carried in, the bagpipes play, and people sit down to have a merry and always memorable feast.

HOLIDAYS THAT REMEMBER PEOPLE IN YOUR FAMILY— INCLUDING YOU!

Huey and Dewey have been making faces at me again. They want to remind me that I seem to have forgotten some very, very important holidays that remember people in your own family. I didn't forget, honest I didn't. I was just saving them for last!

Since 1908 people have set aside the second Sunday in May to celebrate Mother's Day in the United States. But the holiday is celebrated in many other countries of the world, too. For example,

in France Mother's Day is celebrated on the last Sunday in May. But whenever Mother's Day is celebrated, children, according to the old tradition, are very nice to their mother—extra nice, that is. Sometimes they will bring her breakfast in bed or do some of her chores for the day. Lots of children like to give their mother presents on Mother's Day—cards and gifts they have made themselves or saved their money to buy.

Fathers have their day, too. It is held on the third Sunday in June in the United States, where it has been a special day since 1910. On Father's Day children are extra good to their fathers and bring them special gifts and cards—just as they do for their mothers on Mother's Day.

You may be wondering if there is a children's day, too. There are several— not counting your own birthday! In Protestant Church Sunday Schools in the United States, there are special services devoted to children on the second Sunday in June. And, later on, we'll tell you more about Children's Day in Japan, which is held on May 5th. It used to be a holiday for boys only, but now girls are included as well. But it is still the boys who float a huge cloth banner from a pole in front of their house. The banner is shaped like a fish called a carp, and it stands for courage and strength because the carp is a very determined fish.

Universal Children's Day is sponsored by the United Nations. It is celebrated in over 100 countries, generally on the first Monday in October, but the date may vary in different parts of the world. Its purpose is to unite children everywhere in friendship, through special ceremonies and festivities. Huey thinks especially well of this holiday because it is an occasion to honor children. In some countries it has become an official national holiday.

NATIONAL HOLIDAYS

BLOW THE BUGLE; RAISE THE FLAG

Every nation in the world has its special patriotic holidays. Sometimes these holidays commemorate the country's independence or day of liberation; sometimes they celebrate victory in battle or the birth of a famous man.

If there were a calendar showing all the national celebrations around the world, almost every day in the year would be a holiday somewhere. Just to mention a few—Venezuela's national holiday takes place on July 5; the tiny republic of San Marino celebrates on September 3; Afghanistan observes May 27; and Iran October 26. You can learn a great deal about the history of a country just from the patriotic holidays it celebrates.

Patriotic holidays are celebrated differently in different parts of the world. In some countries there are special feasts with favorite foods. In others there are colorful parades and exciting carnivals and fairs. Schools and offices are closed and families get together for a day of fun.

Marchers in Pacific Grove, California, affirm that happiness is a parade!

INDEPENDENCE DAY IN THE UNITED STATES

To the citizens of the United States the most important patriotic holiday of the year is Independence Day, which falls on July 4. Independence Day celebrates a great event in United States history—the signing of the Declaration of Independence by the members of the Continental Congress on July 4, 1776. With this act the 13 colonies broke their ties with Great Britain, declaring themselves a free and independent nation.

You can imagine the excitement as the wonderful news spread. In Philadephia, Pennsylvania, where the document was signed, people cheered and cannons boomed. From the tower of the State House (now Independence Hall) the Liberty Bell rang out, and the statue of King George III was torn down and destroyed. At night bonfires lit the sky, and the streets were crowded with happy people. The festivities continued for several days.

In the following years July 4 was celebrated chiefly by the soldiers of the Revolutionary Army. When the soldiers returned home at the close of the Revolution in 1783, they brought with them

61

The Stars and Stripes flutter against a background of a replica of the United States Constitution.

the idea of a yearly celebration for everyone.

Today the holiday is celebrated with parades, picnics, patriotic speeches, and displays of fireworks. Sometimes Uncle Donald takes the three of us to the beach for a picnic. At night there are beautiful displays of fireworks. July 4 marks the beginning of summer, and everyone joins in the spirit of the holiday.

Many important events have taken place on July 4. In 1802 the United States Military Academy at West Point was officially opened. In 1959 the first 49-star American flag, honoring the new state of Alaska, was raised. The following year, also on July 4, one star was added in honor of the new state of Hawaii. And here's an interesting fact. Two of our country's early presidents, Thomas Jefferson, chief author of the Declaration of Independence, and John Adams, one of its most famous signers, both died on July 4, 1826!

SPECIAL DAYS IN OTHER COUNTRIES

Canada's Dominion Day is celebrated on July 1. In 1867 the provinces of Canada, Nova Scotia, and New Brunswick joined together to form the Dominion of Canada. The act was signed on July 1, and the new Canadian nation was born. Patriotic Canadians honor the anniversary with parades, band concerts, and flag-raising ceremonies. The national anthem, "O Canada," is sung at all gatherings.

63

One of the most festive liberation days in the world is Bastille Day, celebrated in France on July 14. The date marks the destruction of the Bastille, the royal prison, by the people of Paris in 1789, during the French Revolution. To all Frenchmen this event symbolizes the downfall of the monarchy and the beginning of liberty for the people.

Bastille Day celebrations begin on the night before the holiday and last for about 24 hours. In towns and cities bands play patriotic music, and the tricolor, the blue, white, and red flag of France, waves from buildings and housetops. At night monuments and public buildings are brightly lighted, and holiday crowds stroll along the boulevards. There is music and laughter everywhere, and noisy groups dance in the streets till dawn.

FLAGS AND FLOWERS

As members of the Junior Wood-chucks, Huey, Dewey, and I are in charge of the Flag Day ceremonies at our school every June 14. We have a special flag-raising ceremony in the school play-ground, and flags wave from many houses and public buildings. The holiday marks the anniversary of the adoption of the Stars and Stripes as the flag of the United States on June 14, 1777.

Memorial Day is one of the most sacred of America's patriotic holidays. Grandma Duck says that when she was a girl, this holiday was called Decoration Day. It was observed on May 30, as a memorial to Union soldiers who had lost their lives in the Civil War. Now it is observed on the last Monday in May. Memorial Day honors the dead of all wars and many people place flowers on soldiers' graves as a token of love and remembrance. In some of the southern states Confederate Memorial Day is celebrated on April 26.

Right: The American war dead are honored on Memorial Day. Opposite page: The French Army parades on Bastille Day.

65

NO WORK TODAY

Do you know that many countries have special holidays in honor of working people? In the United States, Labor Day is a legal holiday in every state, the District of Columbia, and the territories.

Labor Day was the idea of a carpenter named Peter Maguire who believed that people who worked hard all year should be given some special recognition. An organization called the Knights of Labor held the first Labor Day parade in New York City on September 5, 1882, but it was some time before the holiday was observed in other parts of the country.

In 1894 the United States chose the month of September for Labor Day because it comes midway between July 4 and Thanksgiving, a period during which there were no legal holidays. We always think of Labor Day as the end of summer vacation and the beginning of a new school year.

Above: May Day parade in Red Square, Moscow. The tomb of Lenin, a leader in the Russian Revolution, is in left foreground.
Opposite page: Labor Day parade on New York City's Fifth Avenue.

In many other parts of the world, May 1 is the holiday of the working people. This day is known as International Labor Day. In Latin American countries there are parades and fiestas. Russia held its first May Day celebration in 1891, and for the people of the Soviet Union, May Day is a favorite day for parties and weddings. A military parade is held every May 1 in Red Square, the main square of Moscow, the country's capital.

The United Kingdom—England, Wales, Scotland, and Northern Ireland—observes half a dozen or so holidays called Bank Holidays. They are the equivalent of legal holidays in the United States and Canada. These holidays began in the 1870's for banks only, but now schools, offices, and most businesses are closed and families can spend time together. Different dates are observed in different parts of the United Kingdom, but Good Friday, Easter Monday, a Monday in August, and Boxing day are observed in almost all. Boxing Day has nothing to do with prize-fighting. It is the day after Christmas, when people give gifts to those who have served them during the year.

67

68   *An American family dressed as Pilgrims act out the first Thanksgiving.*

THANKSGIVING DAY

In our travels around the world, Huey, Dewey, and I have taken part in many wonderful holiday celebrations. But one of our favorite holidays is our own Thanksgiving Day. On the fourth Thursday in November we like to be at home with Uncle Donald, Grandma Duck, and the rest of our family to celebrate it. It's a day of warmth and friendship—and of lots of good things to eat.

The first Thanksgiving Day took place in the Plymouth Colony in Massachusetts in the year 1621. After many months of hard work in the fields, a small group of hardy Pilgrims succeeded in reaping their first harvest. Now they could face the cold winter months knowing that there would be plenty of food for all.

Their gratitude at having survived a year of hardship in their new home was so great that the settlers decided to set aside a special time for offering thanks for all their blessings. As one of the men wrote to a friend he had left in England, the small group wanted to "rejoice together after we had gathered the fruits of our labor."

The Pilgrims had many ancient thanksgiving customs to follow. Thousands of years earlier the Greeks and Romans had celebrated the gathering of the harvest, and the custom later spread to many other parts of the world. The Greeks made yearly offerings to Demeter, goddess of the soil, in a 3-day celebration in November. In October the Romans honored the goddess Ceres. They decorated their clothes with fruits and grain, and held sports contests. Ever since those ancient times, people continued to celebrate the harvest with special festivities.

The first American Thanksgiving, over 350 years ago, was a lavish feast. The long table was laden with roast ducks and geese, smoked eel, shellfish, peas, salad greens, and bread. There was delicious wine made from wild grapes.

The guests at the dinner were the Indian chief Massasoit and a band of 90 Wampanoag braves. Several times during the past year there had been conflicts with the Indians, but peace had come at last. The guests brought welcome gifts of game to the feast. The Pilgrim women roasted the waterfowl and wild turkeys on spits over open fires. There were games and singing, and the celebration lasted for 3 days.

The custom of giving thanks for the harvest spread as the country grew. In 1789 George Washington, the first president of the United States, proclaimed November 26 a day of Thanksgiving, but for a long time the holiday continued to be celebrated on different days in different places. Then in 1863, President Abraham Lincoln issued a proclamation calling for one Thanksgiving Day for all the American people. The last Thursday in November was the day chosen.

Today Thanksgiving is celebrated on the fourth Thursday in November. In millions of homes throughout the country there are happy reunions and family feasts. We love the turkey, the cranberries, the sweet potatoes, and the squash —and we wish you could all have a piece of Grandma Duck's delicious pumpkin pie!

Above: Turkey and all the trimmings on Thanksgiving Day!
Opposite page: Disney characters star in Macy's annual Thanksgiving Day parade in New York.

FESTIVALS, HAPPY HOLIDAYS AND CELEBRATIONS

We've saved the best till last. Now we're going to tell you all about festivals and happy holidays. Girls and boys—and ducks—all over the world wait for the fun and the food of these special days.

People in different countries have different festivals. Even when people have the same festivals they may not celebrate them the same way. But one thing is always the same, wherever you are and whatever festival you're celebrating. That's the feeling that it's fun to be alive.

CARNIVAL TIME

First, let me tell you a little secret about holidays. Just something Huey and Dewey and I have noticed. Whenever there's a time of feasting and merry-making, watch out! There's almost sure to be a time of fasting, too, either before or after.

There's a very good example of feasting—and then fasting—in the Christian calendar. It's the tradition for Christians to fast during the period known as Lent —the 40 weekdays before Easter. Ash Wednesday is the beginning of Lent.

In many countries the days just before Ash Wednesday are filled with feasting and fun. This is the gay, noisy, happy time known as carnival.

The word "carnival" comes from the Latin *carnem levare*, which means "to put away meat." Long ago no meat at all was eaten during Lent.

One of the gayest of all carnivals is the New Orleans Mardi Gras in the United States. It was first celebrated in 1857. "Mardi Gras" is French for "fat Tuesday." It is the name that was given long ago to the day before Ash Wednesday. On that day housewives used up all the fats and other foods they would not use during Lent.

The official start of the Mardi Gras season is Epiphany, on January 6. (This is the day, in Christian church history, when the Wise Men presented their gifts to Jesus.)

Opposite page: The Feast of the Stars in the city of Sendai, Japan. It is also celebrated in the rest of Japan, but it takes on special meaning in this region. It is celebrated in August for 2 days, and each household raises bamboo poles decorated with ornaments and long streamers of colored paper.

73

On Epiphany in New Orleans there is a procession with elaborate floats and people in costume. The themes are taken from history or legend. In the evening there are fancy dress balls.

How would you like to fly down to New Orleans with us and see some of the celebrations? In the afternoon and evening of the day before Mardi Gras and of Mardi Gras itself there are more processions and dances. On Monday afternoon Rex, the king of carnival, makes his appearance. He receives the keys to the city from the Mayor. In the early years of the New Orleans Mardi Gras it was the custom to burn a figure representing Rex. Now he just slips off quietly into the crowd.

Grandma Duck told us that one year (it must have been a long time ago) Rex carried her off to his palace. But somehow we find that story hard to believe.

If you think this carnival sounds like fun, how about coming with us down South America way, to the carnival in Rio de Janeiro in Brazil? Months ahead of time people start planning the costumes they will wear at carnival time.

During the celebration the streets are crowded with people—young and old,

Left: Costumed revelers, musicians, and fancy floats are all part of New Orleans' Mardi Gras. Below: Drumbeats and song at Carnival in Brazil's Rio de Janeiro.

rich and poor—all in costume. Songs are written for the occasion and prizes are given for the best ones. Then there's a big costume ball to top off the celebrations.

The three of us are working on a song to sing next year if we can talk Uncle Scrooge into sending us back to Brazil.

Or maybe we should ask him to send us to France. In Nice, in the south of France, people celebrate for two weeks before Ash Wednesday. They battle one another with flowers and follow floats carrying huge figures of the king of carnival and his court of clowns.

75

The carnival in Munich, Germany, is a famous one, too. We wouldn't want you to miss that. It's known as the Fasching. There are parades through the streets, horse-drawn carriages, floats, and costume balls. Even the animals share in the celebration. Dogs are dressed in frilly paper collars and funny little masks for the occasion.

And while we're in Germany let's drop into some of the villages in the south to see the parades. The marchers dress as characters from famous fables and fairy tales. We might even run into paraders who look very much like Uncle Donald and Grandma Duck. We know Uncle Scrooge would feel particularly honored if he knew how many people dress up to look like him.

Right: Folk dancers perform in a public square in Munich, during the pre-Lenten celebration of Fasching.
Opposite page: Oktoberfest in Munich is a gay carnival time that attracts many tourists. The fair grounds are filled with many attractions and popular entertainments.

Many buildings in India, such as this hotel, are illuminated during the Dussehra Festival in October.

INDIA

Now how about packing your bag again and coming with us to celebrate other holidays around the world? Let's take a quick hop over to India, one of the most thickly populated countries in the world. The people of this vast land represent all the major religions. There are Hindus, Buddhists, Christians, and Sikhs. Because of its many different religious beliefs, India probably has a larger number of festivals than any other country.

One of our favorite Indian holidays is Divali, the Festival of Lights, in the fall. Can you guess why we like this celebration so much? You're right—all the children get gifts, and there are fireworks, fairs, special foods, and candy. Houses are decorated with flowers, and little lights are strung on roofs and along the roads.

The lights are intended to guide Lakshmi, Hindu goddess of wealth and good fortune, back to earth. It is said that if Lakshmi visits a home on Divali night the family will have good fortune the following year.

In the spring there's another festival in India. That's Holi, the Fire Festival. It's part of the fun for people to play jokes and tricks on one another, and at night huge bonfires are lighted.

In August a special day is set aside for brothers and sisters. The day is called Raksha Bandhan Day. (The name means "to tie protection.") Brothers give their sisters presents, and each sister ties a scarf, or *rakhi*, around her brother's wrist. That's to protect him from harm in the year ahead.

Above: Slips of paper bearing prayers are often seen tied to trees in the gardens of Japanese temples. Left, above: Paper lanterns used in Japanese memorial services. The lanterns are later carried to the sea and placed in miniature straw boats. Opposite page: Bronze lanterns outside a Japanese temple. Buddhism and Shintoism are Japan's main religions. The two are closely related and often one temple serves both religions.

81

Above: A group of entertainers rehearse for a performance.
Below: Festival time in Kyoto, the ancient capital of Japan, with the streets thronged with people.

Little Japanese girls in front of their doll display during the Feast of Dolls. The dolls represent the Emperor's family and court.

JAPAN

The country that dedicates the most holidays to children is Japan. Oh, how we wish we were Japanese, even for one year, just so we could enjoy these special days!

Children's Day in Japan comes on May 5. Once this festival was set aside for boys, but now it honors girls, too. On this day a pole is set up in the garden of each Japanese house. From the pole floats a huge cloth banner in the shape of an open-mouthed carp. When the wind blows into the carp's mouth, the body of the fish puffs up and floats in the breeze. To the Japanese people the carp is the symbol of such things as strength and courage. During its life cycle this fish

These litle girls are very proud of their beautiful new kimonos. It's an important day for them, in their grown-up clothes and wearing their hair up just like mother!

swims upstream and leaps over waterfalls to lay its eggs. It displays the kind of strength and energy every Japanese father hopes his child will have.

The favorite festival of Japanese girls is the Feast of Dolls that takes place on March 3. The Japanese name for this festival is Hina-Matsuri. This is the day on which girls dress up in their best kimonos and display beautiful, and often quite valuable, dolls for their friends and family. The dolls have been handed down from mother to daughter, sometimes for many generations. The dolls represent emperors and empresses, knights, warriors, and court attendants. After they are displayed they are carefully put away until the next year.

Dragon Boat Festival, Hong Kong.

CHINA

One of the most colorful of all the holidays in China is the Dragon Boat Festival in June. Long narrow boats, called dragon boats—no, Huey, they're not paddled by dragons, they're paddled by men—race one another up and down the rivers. Families stand on the banks, cheering on the crews. One of the special treats of the day is rice dumplings wrapped in leaves.

Another outdoor holiday is a favorite with Chinese children. That's the holiday in the late fall known as the Festival of Climbing the Heights. It's a special day, set aside for flying kites. People start out in the morning with their kites and picnic lunches, and for a whole day kites of all shapes and colors float from every hilltop.

Also in the fall in China there's a celebration called Chung-Ch'iu, in honor of the moon. It's a very poetic, beautiful holiday. People meet in courtyards in the light of the full moon and enjoy the beauty of the evening. There are feasts to the moon, and special cakes, called moon cakes, are served.

Thai priest prepares to fire a rocket during the Nongkai Rocket Festival in Thailand.

THAILAND

If you like to play and splash in the water as much as we do, you'll have to come with us to Thailand in April. We've all been there then, and we can tell you that we had the time of our lives.

The 3-day celebration of Songkran, the Buddhist New Year, begins on April 13. This is the Water Festival, when everyone splashes in the lakes and rivers. People carry buckets of water to wash the statues of the Buddha. There are parades and band concerts, and a Queen of the Water Festival is chosen.

Songkran is also a time when people do good deeds. Birds are set free from their cages and fish are poured from their bowls into the rivers and lakes. Gifts of rice are taken to the temples for the monks.

In the midst of all this, children remember to honor their parents. As a sign of respect, they pour perfumed water onto the hands of their elders.

Captive fish are returned to their watery home during Water Festival in Thailand.

Turkish folk dance.

TURKEY

In Turkey, on April 23, Children's Day is celebrated. This is the anniversary of the first Grand National Assembly in 1920. On this day children are the most important people in the country. They're given free movies and free rides, and a free ball is held in their honor. But best of all, they're permitted to act as government officials. (We wish they'd do that in Duckburg once in a while. We'd have free ice cream and popcorn stands all over.)

Turkey also has another great holiday. This is Seker Bayram, or Candy Holiday. Children dress in costume and pay visits to their relatives. When they arrive they're given gifts of sweets. And just think—if you lived in Turkey, you'd have plenty of time to collect a lot of sweets, because Seker Bayram lasts for 3 days.

87

YUGOSLAVIA

Yugoslavia honors its children with a special holiday called Youth Day, which takes place on May 25th. In all the country's towns and villages, there are children's processions, pageants, and sports contests. Highlights of the holiday are the special exhibits showing work done by young people throughout the year.

NORWAY

Constitution Day in Norway falls on May 17. The weather has warmed up by then and all over the country school children celebrate their national holiday by marching in processions, carrying Norwegian flags. In Oslo, the capital, the king greets the marchers from the balcony of his palace.

A group of Norwegian children in typical costumes surrounds a little "May bride." She wears a small-sized version of the Norwegian country girl's bridal dress and the richly decorated wedding crown with its many pendants.

89

BY THE BEAUTIFUL SEA

Our three holiday hunters next went to Venice, a magnificent city in northeastern Italy built on a lagoon of the Adriatic Sea. From the Middle Ages to the end of the 18th century, Venice was a major sea power and center of trade between East and West. On Ascension Day in August each year the people of Venice renew the "marriage" of their city to the sea in a great public ceremony.

In olden times, Venice's leader, the doge, boarded his beautifully decorated state barge and with a fleet of other boats sailed to the meeting place of Venice's lagoon and the sea. There the doge threw a golden wedding ring that had been blessed by the Church into the sea and said, "O, Sea we wed thee in sign of our true and everlasting dominion." Choirs sang, guns boomed, and Venetians cheered. And even today the people of Venice renew their city's vows of marriage to the sea in the same fashion.

Above and opposite page: Several moments from the "marriage of the sea" ceremony in Venice, Italy.

WHEN KNIGHTS ARE BOLD

Huey, Dewey, and Louie were so excited by the historic ceremony in Venice that they decided to visit another town in Italy called Arezzo. Arezzo is notable for its beautiful cathedral and for being the birthplace of the famous Guido d'Arezzo, who invented the modern system of musical notation. It is a city where the past lives on in many ways.

On the first Sunday in September, for example, the whole town joins in celebrating the past by holding a medieval tournament called a joust. In a joust two teams imitated medieval forms of warfare, observing very strict rules. In fact some people say our traditions of fair play and respect for the rules of a game come from these medieval tournaments.

In Arezzo men train all year to represent their part of town in the joust. On the holiday itself they wear colorful 13th-century costumes as they parade to the cathedral to have their weapons blessed. Then they go on foot and on horseback to joust with such ancient arms as halberds, lances, and swords. For one day all Arezzo is a living monument to the past.

Every year the people of Arezzo, Italy, recreate the pageantry, splendor, and excitement of a medieval tournament, as the scenes on these two pages show. A tournament is a way of staging a war as it was waged in the Middle Ages but without bloodshed.

BULLFIGHTS AND BONFIRES

"You know," said Louie, "I think we had some of our best holiday fun in Spain." Huey and Dewey agreed, of course, as would anyone who has ever been to one of the gigantic holiday celebrations in that country.

One of the most famous events is the Fiesta of San Fermin, which is held each year between July 6 and 20, in the city of Pamplona in northern Spain. Although the holiday celebrates San Fermin, you learn in only a few minutes there that the stars of the show are bulls. On the first day of the fiesta the bulls are allowed to run through the narrow streets to the bullring.

In the forefront are some of the bravest young men in the world, running at a fast clip to show their courage—and to avoid being trampled by the running, snorting,

94

Above: With swirling skirts and clicking fingers, Spanish folk dancers perform traditional dances.
Opposite page: A young boy dressed as a Spanish cavalier serves as a coachman during a festival in Seville, Spain.

stomping bulls. Then, throughout the fiesta period, there are bullfights, fireworks, and everywhere the sound of haunting Spanish music.

You will hear more lovely Spanish music at the *Falla de San Chusep*, or Festival of St. Joseph, in Valencia. It begins on March 13 and reaches its great climax on March 19, St. Joseph's Day. In the Valencian dialect of Spanish, *falla* means bonfire, and bonfires are the way the Valencians celebrate this holiday and welcome spring. All week you can see giant carved figures representing all kinds of comic characters. The best designed figure is placed in a museum. The rest are burned in the great bonfire on March 19th, while firecrackers explode and everyone cheers.

95

A SMALL NATION'S GIANT HOLIDAYS

Huey, Dewey, and Louie all agreed that Belgium had some of the most unusual holidays in Europe. "Remember the Festival of the Cats at Ypres?" Louie asked. "That's the holiday that recalls the time the Belgians became Christians and gave up their worship of the goddess Freya who traveled in a catdrawn chariot." Our holiday experts had heard that in the old days real cats were thrown from the bell tower to symbolize the end of Freya-worship. Now stuffed animals are thrown to the laughing crowd and giant cat puppets are drawn through the streets.

Speaking of giants, hardly a Belgian holiday parade is complete without its magnificently dressed 12-foot-high puppets.

Above: One of a procession of giants that can be seen in Ath, Belgium, during the holiday at the end of August is La Gouyasse. Opposite page: Bayard, Roland's horse, the star of the parade. Over 21 feet high, it is ridden by four children who represent the four sons of Aymon. Bayard is moved by 15 men who are hidden inside the horse's trappings.

97

HOLIDAYS ON HORSEBACK

"Another colorful holiday," said Louie, "that has been celebrated for centuries, is the horse race called the *palio*. It is held on the main square in Siena, Italy, in July and August each year. The race, which is held in honor of the Virgin, is called the *palio* because that is the Italian word for the brocaded banner that is the prize. Ten horses run in the race, each representing a *contrada*, or district, of Siena. Age-old rivalries between the different districts come to life each year as they bring out their traditional costumes and banners for the race.

"Thousands of Italians and visitors from all over the world crowd into the stands to hear the roll of drums that signals the opening of the race. Next come matched black horses carrying uniformed officers bearing the flag of Siena. They are followed by workmen in medieval costumes and boys twirling and tossing bright banners in the air. Another roll of drums and the race begins as jockeys dressed in medieval costumes spur their horses to victory. The winning district keeps the *palio* in its church for a year to honor the Virgin."

Excitement fills the air during the palio in Siena, Italy. Before the horse races begin, the streets are packed with people hurrying to the main square of the city to watch the competition between the various districts of Siena. Victory is eagerly sought and rivalry runs high. The palio is an important tourist attraction, and people come to Siena from all over the world to witness this event, which had its beginning in the Middle Ages.

SOME INDIAN CEREMONIES

"In some places," Louie reminded his brothers, "old traditions and ceremonies are disappearing. Think about how the way of life of the North American Indians has changed. Because many Indians have moved away from their old homes, they no longer celebrate as they used to when their ancestors lived as farmers, hunters, and nomads."

"That's too bad," said Huey and Dewey together. "Can't we see any Indian ceremonies any more?"

"Yes," said Louie, "some of the traditions are kept alive on Indian reservations all over the country. We have to imagine some of the others from descriptions we have of them.

"Let's pretend it is a cold night on the high plains of the west," Louie said, "and watch some Crow Indian men dressed in buffalo skins and wearing buffalo-head masks. They dance around a fire until they get word from a scout that a herd of buffalo is near. The Crow believed that

100

the magic of their dance made the buffalo they needed for food and clothing appear.

"In the olden days," Louie went on, "some Indians of the northwest had great feasts of giving called potlatches. It was a source of honor to one's family to serve the most food and to give the most presents to its guests. Another festival marked by gift giving was held by the Hopi Indians of the southwest. Good spirits called Cloud People gave presents to all the little children." Huey and Dewey, looking very smart said, "I'll bet those good spirits were really fathers dressed to look like Cloud People." And of course they were right.

"There were ceremonies of thanksgiving, too," Louie went on. "After each harvest the Indians thanked the gods for their goodness in providing rain for the seeds to grow. The Iroquois Indians even wore special corn-husk masks for this autumn celebration that honored the gods of olden times."

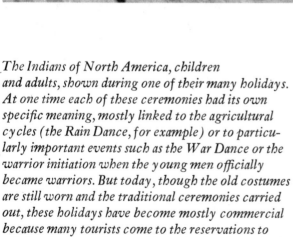

The Indians of North America, children and adults, shown during one of their many holidays. At one time each of these ceremonies had its own specific meaning, mostly linked to the agricultural cycles (the Rain Dance, for example) or to particularly important events such as the War Dance or the warrior initiation when the young men officially became warriors. But today, though the old costumes are still worn and the traditional ceremonies carried out, these holidays have become mostly commercial because many tourists come to the reservations to admire the descendants of Sitting Bull and watch their mysterious dances.

101

102

THREE CHEERS FOR FREEDOM

In the Latin American countries Indian and European traditions live on side by side. Huey, Dewey, and Louie knew this from their visit to Bolivia on its Independence Day. The Bolivians won their freedom from the Spanish king at the battle of Ayacucho in 1824. Then on August 6, 1825, the Republic of Bolivia was born and that's the day when they still celebrate their independence. Each year on that day Indians wear their best costumes.

"Venezuela's Independence Day is celebrated on July 5th with much more solemn ceremonies," Louie said. "It seemed to me that every family in the country took part in rites recalling the signing of the Declaration of Independence from Spain in 1811. The Venezuelan flag was flying everywhere, especially in the capital, Caracas, where the biggest parades and most speeches are given. There were gorgeous floats and terrific bands playing.

"Yes," said Huey, "But remember the day we almost lost our voices in Mexico?" "Sure," answered Dewey. "We were in Mexico at midnight September 15th when the Mexican people shout for freedom. This recalls the shout that began the Mexican Revolution in the 19th century. Even today every Mexican still sings out, 'Long live the Virgin of Guadalupe. Long live Independence! Death to the Gachupines [Spanish].'"

"Do you remember," asked Louie, "how the President of Mexico shouted these words from his balcony. They have the right idea in Mexico. Freedom is something to shout about!"

Bolivians celebrate Independence Day. Unlike countries where national holidays are celebrated only with military parades, Independence Day in Bolivia gives the people a chance to get together with dances, costume parades, and masked balls.

103

A TIME FOR FEASTING

Huey, Dewey, and I were a little bit hoarse and very hungry after celebrating all those independence days. We thought we should just sit back and remember some of the great feasts we had in Greece and in the Soviet Union at Easter time.

At the end of the solemn Lenten season in all the Christian countries of the world, there are great celebrations to commemorate Easter. In the countries where most people belong to the Eastern Orthodox Church the celebration seems somehow to be especially colorful—and very delicious too!

In Greece the Easter meal begins with eggs that have been dyed red. Next comes an unusual soup called *mayiritsa*, which is made of the innards of the Easter lamb cooked with rice and dill. Then there is a green salad with sardines followed by the roast lamb. Nobody is ever too sleepy after this huge meal to go to Easter dances or visit friends and neighbors.

The people of the Soviet Union and many Eastern European countries make the Easter season the greatest holiday of the year. During the bleak, cold days of late February or early March these Slavic people celebrate the days before Lent and the 40-day fast with Maslenitsa. This is the butter festival when they eat thin pancakes dripping with butter. Toward the end of the Lenten fast the women start to bake the high yeast cakes filled with raisins and nuts called *kulich*. Often the cakes are iced or decorated with candles and flowers and then taken to the church to be blessed.

Kulich is the dessert that closes the enormous Easter dinner. The dinner begins with *zakuska* (appetizers) and includes ham baked in dough, sausage, cold duck, chicken salad, and of course the elaborate and beautifully painted Easter eggs. It is a memorable meal celebrating the most sacred of Christian holy days and the beginning of spring.

Above: Easter service at the Greek Orthodox Church in Jerusalem. Left: Folk dancers in Megara, Greece, await their turn to perform.

105

GOLDEN DAYS AND WEEKS

Huey, Dewey, and I kept going back to Japan because there were so many exciting festivals there. We especially enjoyed Golden Week in May. It begins with the celebration of the Emperor's Birthday on April 29th, a national holiday, when the Imperial Palace in Tokyo is opened to the public. During Golden Week many businesses close and the Japanese travel around their country. The next holiday in this week of holidays is May Day on May 1st. It is followed on May 3 by Constitution Day. On that day the Japanese celebrate the writing of their new democratic laws at the end of World War II.

We told you earlier about some of the special Japanese days for children, but Huey just reminded me that on November 15th there is the Seven-Five-Three Festival. Parents take their daughters age 7 and 3 and their sons age 5 and 3 to the shrine. They celebrate the fact that their children of these ages have lived through what Japanese used to think were the most dangerous years. It is a great day for the children because they are given new kimonos and sometimes new costumes such as a spaceman's suit!

An exciting event is the Tsurugaoka Hachiman Festival in Kamakura in September. During this 2-day holiday there are processions, ceremonial dances in the shrines, and archery contests. In the contests, archers mounted on horseback gallop by targets and compete to see who is able to hit the bull's-eye most often. We wanted to see what kind of sharpshooters we were, but it was all we could do to stay on the horse, let alone shoot an arrow!

Kite flying is a popular sport in Japan.

106

A Japanese girl helps her mother decorate their home for the New Year.

AFRICAN HOLIDAYS

Huey and Dewey have just reminded me that I have forgotten to tell you about some of the wonderful holidays and ceremonies we have seen in Africa.

We felt quite at home in Liberia, which is in the western region of Africa. With the help of the American Colonization Society, Liberia gained its independence in 1847. Its capital city, Monrovia, is named for the American President James Monroe. We were in Monrovia on Independence Day, July 26th, in time to hear the 21-gun salute that begins the holiday and to see the great parade that follows. We heard Liberia's president speak and then went to a special party that is held just for children on that day. Liberia is really a home away from home for Americans. The Liberians even celebrate Thanksgiving as a national holiday in November in memory of the first American colonists who landed there in November, 1820.

In some parts of Africa much older customs are still observed. In Ghana a Coming of Age ceremony is held for young girls when they reach the age for marriage. Among the Fanti people in southern Ghana two girls accompany the bride-to-be from house to house in the village to make it known that she is ready for marriage.

At Oginibo in western Nigeria there is a day-long holiday for brides. The girls are dressed in the most beautiful clothes that can be made and wear treasured gold necklaces and earrings. As the procession of brides moves to the village shrine, all the people cheer them. The bridegrooms join their brides under a great canopy. Surrounding the couples are bridesmaids wearing only strings of coral beads around their waists. Everyone offers a sacrifice to the goddess of weddings and everyone praises the brides. The day ends with great banquets honoring the newlyweds.

We would have enjoyed staying longer in Africa but other celebrations were still to be seen.

Towering headdresses sweep through the air as Dogon dancers of Sanga, in the West African nation of Mali, perform a ritual dance.

Berbers from the village of Tinezouline, Morocco, celebrate their country's Independence Day. On following pages: A picturesque procession in Ethiopia celebrates Epiphany.

HALLOWEEN

We've been talking about some of our favorite holidays in other parts of the world. But there are many interesting holidays right here in the United States. When it comes to having fun, there's no better holiday than Halloween. It's a time for playing games, dressing up in costumes, and having parties. Uncle Donald always carves a Halloween jack-o'-lantern out of a pumpkin for us.

The name Halloween comes from All Hallows' Even, a religious holiday. Centuries ago the Catholic Church set aside November 1 as All Saints' or All Hallows' Day. The night before was called All Hallows' Even (another word for eve or evening). This was later shortened to Halloween.

But the customs of Halloween go back long before that, to the days of ancient Gaul and Britain. In those days there were priests called druids. The druids believed that witches, demons, and all sorts of evil spirits roamed the earth on the night before November 1. People were quite frightened of these evil spirits. They armed themselves and built giant bonfires to frighten them away. The druids had other ways of dealing with the evil spirits. They put out food offerings, hoping these "treats" would make the spirits friendlier. They also tried to trick the demons by dressing up as witches themselves. After all, one witch   113 wouldn't be likely to harm another witch!

Huey, Dewey, and I love to dress up in spooky costumes on Halloween. Huey pretends to be a witch. He puts on a pointed black hat, a black cape, and one of those scary witch's masks. Dewey likes to turn himself into a black cat—which isn't easy for a little duck to do! But he puts on long cat's ears made of cardboard and cat's whiskers made of pieces of string. Why he almost fools me! Some years I dress up as a ghost. I wear a white sheet and a pumpkin head with the eyes, ears, nose, and mouth cut out.

Then we go out to "trick or treat." We visit friends and relatives and get lots of candy and fruit. Grandma Duck always has a big basket of oranges and bananas waiting for us when we arrive—enough to last for weeks!

But we've also added something new to our tricking and treating. Instead of just collecting lots of sweets for ourselves, we do something for other people as well. Like many other boys and girls, we ask our neighbors to contribute money to UNICEF—the United Nations Children's Emergency Fund. We have special UNICEF boxes for them to put their dimes and quarters in. Most people are happy to help this good cause. The money we collect is sent to UNICEF headquarters and is used to aid needy children all over the world.

Besides tricking and treating, we generally go to a party on Halloween. It's always lots of fun. One game that we like very much is called ducking for apples. All you need is a large pan filled with water and some apples. Each person kneels by the pan with his hands behind his back. He must pick up the apple using only his teeth. Of course, with our duck's bills we are very good at this game—and we don't mind getting our faces wet.

Opposite page: A group of delightful French puppets designed by André Tahon. The star of the group (at left, below Harlequin) is Papotin.

114

French women model their fancy hats in observance of St. Catherine's Day.

APRIL FOOL!

A few weeks ago Huey, Dewey, and I were sitting in school waiting for our teacher to arrive. Suddenly one of our classmates came in and said, "Our teacher is sick and we're not going to have any school today!" Well, we all got up and started for the door. But just as we got there, our classmate laughed and called out "April Fool!"

I guess we've all had April Fool jokes played on us at one time or another. No one knows exactly when this custom started. But the idea of April 1st as a day for practical jokes has been around for a long time.

In France, April 1st is called *poisson d'avril*, which means "April fish." On this day, French children who play tricks sometimes receive a chocolate fish as a gift. Grownups also play tricks on each other—but they don't get candy fish.

SAINT CATHERINE'S DAY

November 25th is a special day in France for ladies who are over 25 and aren't married. On that day, the French observe Saint Catherine's Day. Saint Catherine is the patron saint of unmarried women. On November 25, she is supposed to bless all the single girls so that they will find husbands in the coming year.

There are usually parades, dances, and lots of parties on Saint Catherine's Day. Many girls follow the old custom of putting on special clothes to celebrate the holiday. They wear white aprons and fancy hats that are made especially for this day.

ARBOR DAY

About 100 years ago a man named J. Sterling Morton looked at the landscape of his home state of Nebraska and saw that there were hardly any trees—just open prairie and hills. Mr. Morton had an idea. Why not set aside one day each year for planting trees? He told others about his idea, and they agreed. Morton's idea was so successful that more than 1,000,000 trees were planted in Nebraska during the first year. Other states quickly adopted the plan. Soon tens of thousands of new trees were springing up across the nation.

Every state in the Union now has a day for planting trees. It is known as Arbor Day. The date for Arbor Day varies from state to state. For example, Nebraska's Arbor Day falls on April 22, Mr. Morton's birthday. In many of the southern states the date is sometime between December and February. That's the best time for planting trees in the south. But in the north, Arbor Day is observed in the springtime—usually in April or May.

The holiday is also celebrated in Canada and in other countries of the world. Many schools devote the week of Arbor Day to special conservation programs. Students are encouraged to plant trees and to take part in activities to protect forests, wildlife, and parks.

A family tree-planting on Arbor Day.

VALENTINE'S DAY

Every February 14, we make a large greeting card shaped like a heart. Then we get some flowers and candy and take them to Grandma Duck. She's always thrilled with these gifts—especially since Uncle Scrooge hates to buy presents even on Valentine's Day.

This holiday is believed to have had its beginning in ancient Roman times. Every year on February 15, the Romans held a festival known as the Lupercalia. During this festival the Roman men wore the names of the girls who were to be their partners pinned to their sleeves. We still say of a young man in love that "he wears his heart on his sleeve."

When Christianity became widespread, the Church changed the festival into a religious holiday. It was moved back to February 14, and called Saint Valentine's Day—in honor of a Roman priest named Valentine who was killed because of his Christian beliefs.

Will this little woodchuck see its shadow?

WHAT'S THE WEATHER?

The weather on certain days, according to legend, is a clue to the kind of weather that's ahead of us. We can't promise you that a look at the sky on these days will really tell you what kind of weather to expect, but it's worth a try.

GROUNDHOG DAY

Groundhog Day is one of these special weather-predicting days. Another name for groundhog is woodchuck, and as members of the Junior Woodchucks, Huey, Dewey, and I take special pride in Groundhog Day.

In the United States, on February 2, people watch for the groundhog to wake up from its winter's nap and come outside and stretch. If the sun is shining and the groundhog can see its shadow, we can all expect 6 more weeks of winter. If it's a cloudy day, we can look forward to an early spring. Or so the story goes.

119

SAINT SWITHIN'S DAY

Another day that's related to the weather is Saint Swithin's Day, July 15. If it rains on that day in England, people expect to use their umbrellas for the next 40 days. (Of course, a rainy Saint Swithin's Day doesn't scare us ducks.) But if it's sunny on July 15, the English look forward to 40 days of fair, dry weather.

There is a famous legend about Saint Swithin, a humble British monk who lived more than 1,000 years ago. According to the story, he asked to be buried outside Winchester Cathedral, where the rain would fall on his grave.

When he died, his wish was granted. But about 100 years later, on July 15, 971, some monks decided to honor his memory by moving his body inside the cathedral. On that day torrents of rain fell. And the rain continued for 40 days. Everyone thought that Saint Swithin was so angered at being moved he had sent the rain. The project had to be given up.

However, some years later, the saint's remains were moved and placed in a tomb inside the cathedral. And believe it or not, that day there was no rain.

Opposite page: Winchester Cathedral in Winchester, England, was founded nearly 900 years ago. It is 500 feet in length, which makes it the longest Gothic-style cathedral in all of Europe.

SAINT MARTIN'S DAY

Saint Martin's Day, November 11, is a lovely autumn children's holiday celebrated in many European countries. If the weather is sunny on Saint Martin's Day the winter ahead is supposed to be cold. If there is a frost before Saint Martin's Day, the winter should be mild.

The holiday honors Saint Martin, who, according to legend, was known for his extreme modesty. When he was named Bishop of Tours, he felt himself so unworthy of the honor that he tried to hide in a coop full of geese. But the flapping of their wings gave him away. And so, because the geese betrayed him, goose is the delicacy served at Saint Martin's Day dinners.

Long ago on Saint Martin's Eve people lighted huge bonfires and children marched in torchlight parades singing songs to the saint. Today, in parts of Austria, young people walk through the woods by candlelight. They beat noisemakers and call on the spirits of winter.

In France and Germany the annual feast of the new wine takes place on Saint Martin's Day. Children fill buckets with water and ask Saint Martin to change the water to wine. And the miracle really happens! (The three of us are in on the secret, but you must promise not to tell. It's not a miracle at all. The wine is put in the buckets by the parents.) Everyone eats sweets called Saint Martin's horns.

In parts of Belgium children make lanterns out of squashes and watermelons and march with noisemakers and horns to celebrate this holiday. English children wander through the streets of the towns asking for gifts of apples and nuts. Then they thank the donors by singing a song about Saint Martin, a good old man who repays every gift.

And now, boys and girls, it's time for us to sing our song of thanks to you. Thank you for coming around the world with us on our great holiday adventure. Don't forget us—we'll never forget you and the fun we've had together. The Junior Woodchucks salute you—and say good-bye. We hope every day is as happy as a holiday for you.

Huey, Dewey, and Louie

Roast goose is the traditional dinner eaten on St. Martin's Day in many European countries. Do you think this boy's goose will be cooked?

123

INDEX

Note: Page numbers in italics refer to pictures

126